HEALING AND FREEDOM

Restoring the Foundations

Healing and Freedom

© Restoring the Foundations, 2016. All Rights Reserved.

Restoring the Foundations
2849 Laurel Park Highway
Hendersonville, NC 28739
828-696-9075
office@restoringthefoundations.org
20161102

Bible quotes are from several Bible versions

AMP   *The Amplified Bible*. Copyright by Zondervan Publishing House, 1965, Grand Rapids, Michigan. All Rights Reserved.

MSG   Scripture taken from "The Message." Copyright 1993, 1994, 1995, 1996, 2000, 2001, 2002. Used by permission of NavPress Publishing Group.

NAS   *New American Standard* Bible. Copyright THE LOCKMAN FOUNDATION, 1960, 1962, 1963, 1968, 1971, 1973, 1975, 1977. A corporation not for profit. La Habra, California. All Rights Reserved.

NIV   *The Holy Bible, New International Version*. Copyright 1973, 1978, 1984, by the International Bible Society. All Rights Reserved.

NKJV   "Scripture taken from the New King James Version. Copyright © 1982 by Thomas Nelson, Inc. Used by permission. All rights reserved."

NLT   Holy Bible. New Living Translation. Copyright © 1996 by Tyndale Charitable Trust. Used by permission of Tyndale House Publishers.

First Edition, 2016.

Contents

Dear Reader,

This book is a brief introduction to the ministry of Restoring the Foundations. It is not intended to be an in-depth explanation of the ministry. The complete and thorough explanation of Restoring the Foundations ministry is found in the book *Restoring the Foundations 2nd Edition* by Chester and Betsy Kylstra. This book can be purchased from our online store found at **www.RestoringTheFoundations.org.**

We believe that all people can benefit greatly from receiving RTF ministry.

- You may be a Pastor who is considering introducing RTF in your church, but you want to experience the ministry personally first.
- You may desire to go deeper with the Lord and yet not be aware of any specific issues at work in your life.
- You may have a good relationship with the Lord but you want all that God has and you want to grow even more.
- You may recognize your need for healing or know someone that you feel would benefit from Restoring the Foundations ministry.

If you relate to any of these statements, then this book will help give you a simple overview of Restoring the Foundations Ministry. For a more thorough explanation please order the Restoring the Foundations book listed above.

It is our goal to help people experience greater intimacy with Father God and really enjoy the abundant life here and now.

If you want to find out more about ministry or training you'll find the contact information in the back of the book along with information about our founders, Chester and Betsy Kylstra.

"The Spirit of the Sovereign Lord is upon me, for the Lord has anointed me to bring good news to the poor. He has sent me to comfort the brokenhearted and to proclaim that captives will be released and prisoners will be freed."

Isaiah 61:1 (New Living Translation)

Introduction

You are embarking on an adventure! An adventure has a destination, but there are usually unexpected twists and turns along the way. Your destination is freedom! The pathway to freedom through Restoring the Foundations Ministry is clear. The exciting part is that as we trust the Holy Spirit's leading, healing comes. As healing is experienced, then freedom from those things in the past that have held you back is also realized.

You may be grateful for the growth you have experienced in your relationship with God, but perhaps you hunger for more. Restoring the Foundations Ministry is an excellent way to step into an even deeper walk with the Lord. It can also greatly impact many areas of your life, including your relationships.

We want to encourage you to jump into the Preparation for Ministry process with both feet, determined to experience all the freedom and healing that Jesus died to give you.

"The thief comes only to steal and kill and destroy; I came that they may have life, and have it abundantly." John 10:10.

You have an enemy, satan, and he has been trying to destroy you. It has been his purpose to bring destruction into your life. He has robbed you of joy and of the promises that God gives. He has stolen your true God-given identity and has lied to you about who you are. He has tried to kill your God-given destiny. Jesus died to set you free from your past, to heal you from your wounds and to give you abundant life now.

"He has sent me to proclaim release to the captives,
And recovery of sight to the blind,
To set free those who are oppressed." Luke 4:18

Are you sick and tired of feeling like you are on a merry-go-round and that the same issues keep popping up, hindering you from being all that you know God intended for you? Are you ready to say, "Enough is enough?" Then it's time for war! It's time to get ready to kick the enemy in the teeth as you take back the land of your life!

"Other people are going to find healing in your wounds. Your greatest life messages and your most effective ministry will come out of your deepest hurts."
Rick Warren

Your life will change as you experience amazing healing that comes through Him. As you commit to reading this book, and allow God to prepare your heart, you will be tilling up the ground that will bring forth the fruit of healing and freedom.

The ministry of Restoring the Foundations (RTF) was founded on the revelation given to Chester and Betsy Kylstra. Since that time, thousands of people have received healing by going through Restoring the Foundations ministry. It changed our lives and we believe that it will also change yours. We are excited for you to experience true healing and freedom as you encounter the love of the Father and embrace all that Jesus Christ died to give you.

Healing Hearts, Changing Lives, Transforming Nations and empowering others to do the same is what Restoring the Foundations is all about.

Blessings,

Lee and Cindi Whitman
Executive Directors
Restoring the Foundations

4

What Is Restoring the Foundations?

Many people in the world are trapped, wounded, and believe they are helpless. We were once among that group. By the Grace of God, we were given a revelation of significant keys of the Kingdom that enabled first us, and then many others, to receive God's healing, deliverance, and freedom. This book reveals the keys needed to unlock the chains that bind our lives and block and hinder our Christian growth.

These keys are the revelation of how to minister to four problem areas that are in all our lives, and the importance of ministering to all of these problem areas simultaneously. When we minister to Sins of the Fathers and Resulting Curses, Ungodly Beliefs, Soul/Spirit Hurts, and Demonic Oppression at the same time, we call this **An Integrated Approach to Healing Ministry**.

God has shown us that each of these four areas are interconnected to and strengthened by each of the other three. If we ignore any one of these problem areas when we are either receiving ministry or ministering to someone, we leave an open door for the enemy to undermine the entire healing process. Obviously, we don't want to do that!

Let's take a brief look at these four problem areas.

Sins of the Fathers and Resulting Curses -
Dealing with Life's Baggage

This problem area is rooted in the second commandment (Ex 20:3-6) where the sin of idolatry results in the curse of "the iniquities of the fathers being visited upon the children unto the third and fourth generations." In order to get free of this curse, God provides a pattern of confession that we can follow, first mentioned in Lev 26:40. We confess our ancestors' sin as well as our own sin (1 John 1:9); we forgive as needed (Matthew 6:14-15); appropriate, or receive for ourselves, Christ's finished work on the Cross to break curses (Galatians 3:13); and, we recover the "legal ground" from the enemy (Colossians 2:14).

Ungodly Beliefs – Renewing the Mind

Our minds are full of untruths and half-truths inherited from our ancestors (i.e., parents, grandparents) and formed from the hurtful circumstances and experiences of our own lives and our culture. These Ungodly Beliefs need to be changed into Godly Beliefs (Romans 12:2). This is accomplished through a carefully structured procedure of repentance for believing lies, renouncing the lies, and receiving God's truth to renew our minds. This also recovers "legal ground" as we break our agreements with demons.

Soul/Spirit Hurts - Healing Life's Hurts

Jesus came to heal the brokenhearted (Luke 4:18). As we "wait upon the Lord" and prayerfully listen to Him, He is eager to come and heal the hurts of our soul and spirit. He does this by showing us the original causes of our hurts. Then, after we take care of necessary forgiveness, releasing, and renouncing, He heals what He has revealed. All "legal ground" given to the enemy from our sinful responses to the hurts, as well as the inherited legal ground, is recovered as a part of the ministry.

Demonic Oppression – Freedom from Oppression

After ministering to the above three problem areas, it is now relatively easy to disassemble and destroy the Demonic Oppression (Mark 16:17) and eliminate them from our lives since they have lost their "legal ground." It is a delight for the Ministry Team help others gain this freedom.

The Restoring the Foundations Integrated Approach to Healing Ministry releases healing into our lives that is often profound and permanent. This can be a major life-changing occurrence. We experience the transforming power of God's grace and love as His purpose is accomplished and we are conformed more and more into the image of His Dear Son, Jesus Christ. This further opens the door for intimate fellowship with God and His empowerment, making it possible for us to live the "overcoming" Christian life.

In the following chapters we present the sources of our four problem/ministry areas in detail so that we may be better equipped both to receive ministry and to minister more effectively to others. Before we look at these, however, let's look at two foundational truths which undergird this Integrated Approach to Healing Ministry.

Restoring the Foundations

"TO HEAR GOD'S VOICE
we must turn down
the world's volume."

unknown

Hearing God's Voice

An important aspect of receiving our healing and continuing to grow in the Lord involves hearing God's Voice. Did you know that God desires to speak to you on a daily basis; to be your counselor and friend; and to provide guidance, peace, correction, and direction?

John 16:12-15 *"I have many more things to say to you, but you cannot bare them now. But when He, the Spirit of truth comes, He will guide you into all truth; for He will not speak on His own initiative, but whatever He hears, He will speak; and He will disclose to you what is to come. He shall glorify Me for He shall take of Mine, and shall disclose it to you. All things that the Father has are Mine; therefore I said, that He takes of Mine, and will disclose it to you".* (NAS)

John 10:27, *"My sheep hear My voice, and I know them, and they follow Me."*

Some ways that God can speak to us:

- **Audible voice** - God rarely speaks in this manner, but there are a few times recorded in Scripture where He spoke audibly. This occurs when we literally hear God speak to us, just as our friends speaks to us (1 Samuel 3:10, Acts 9:3-7).

- **Still Small Voice** - This is one of the most common ways God speaks to us. It comes as a sense of knowing or a whisper from deep inside. We may not have recognized this as God's Voice and may have ignored it in the past. Sometimes people think that it is just their conscience speaking or label it a hunch or intuition (1 Kings 19:12, John 14:26).

- **Dreams** - When we wonder if a dream is from the Lord, we can ask Him for wisdom and discernment. God speaks in this way sometimes when we will not slow down during the day to listen to His voice. Dreams that are from the Lord need be interpreted carefully (Genesis 15:1, 20:3, Daniel 2, Joel 2:28, Acts 2:17).

- **Inward Vision** - This is when we experience God's communication through seeing a picture in our spirit. God creates the image within our minds and spirits (Habakkuk 1, John 5:19-20, 8:38-40, Acts 2:17-18, Joel 2:28).

- **Praying in the Spirit with Interpretation** - Interpretation of tongues is one of the nine gifts of the Spirit listed in 1 Corinthians 12. Sometimes as we speak in other tongues, God may reveal to us what we are praying. This is also a way God speaks to the church through tongues and interpretation (1 Corinthians 14:5-6, Romans 8:26-27).

- **Word of Knowledge, Wisdom and Discernment** - The information might be a fact (Word of Knowledge) or how to deal with a situation in the form of a plan or strategy (Word of Wisdom). It could also be a discernment of spiritual information. Discernment of Spirits is the supernatural ability to know what spiritual influence is at work (1 Corinthians. 12:7-11, Hebrews 5:14).

- **Illumination of Scripture** - This occurs when God is communicating with us by making the Logos (written word- The Bible) become a Rhema word, a personal word that speaks directly to us and our situation. It may seem like the words are leaping right off the page. Excitement and comfort usually follow. God can use this method to reveal either how to apply this Scripture to a specific situation or to give the reader a deeper understanding of the passage. Those called to be teachers frequently experience hearing God's voice in this way (Psalm 119:105,125,130).

- **Seeing His Words In Our Spirit** - This is another form of an inward vision, but instead of seeing pictures, a person sees words. The words can be anything. They can be someone's name, an address, a phone number or a sentence (Genesis 6:14-22).

- **Personal Prophecy** - This communication occurs when someone speaks a specific, individual, personal word that he is sensing from the Lord to another person. The word conveys God's heart, mind, and counsel for that person (1 Corinthians 14:5-6, 24-25).

- **Song of the Lord** - This is the singing of a personal prophecy from the Lord (1 Chronicles 25:1-2, 5, 7).

How to hear from God:

Preparation - To hear from God on a daily basis, it is important to prepare. Preparation involves:

- Being in a relationship with Jesus Christ (John 10:14 - My sheep hear My voice…).

- Growing in the Word, renewing your mind in the Word of God so that we develop the mind of Christ (Romans 12:2, 1 Corinthians 13:6).

- Quickly repenting of any sin (Psalm 32:3-11, 139:23).

- Having pen and paper out so that we can record what God is speaking to us (Habakkuk 2).

Atmosphere - Are we creating an atmosphere in which we hear from God?

- Have an attitude of worship, trust and faith.

- Be still and know that He is God (Psalm 46:10). If our minds are distracted and crowded with other things, it will be hard to hear God's voice and be clear on what He is speaking to us.

- Fix our eyes on Jesus, not on our own desires (Hebrews 12:2). If our eyes are on our own desires, then we may miss what God is truly saying to us (Matthew 6:32-33).

- Seek God in humility. Want His will over our own just as Jesus did in prayer in the Garden of Gethsemane (Luke 22:39, 2 Chronicles 7:14, 1 Peter 5:6).

Receiving - We may see images in our spirit or hear the still small voice.

- Write down what we believe He is saying to us. Don't analyze at this time. Otherwise, we will remain in "head" mode and not be listening with our heart. Just go ahead and write it all down. We can analyze and evaluate it after we have finished listening.

Once our prayer/listening time with the Lord is over, there are several things to do to evaluate whether we heard from God or from some other source.

After we finish listening, it is good to:

- Praise God for speaking to us.

- Look over what we have written and see if it is in alignment with the Word or if it is contradicting the Bible. If we have been developing the mind of Christ, we may be able to tell immediately if it is in alignment with the Word from our knowledge of the Scriptures.

- Much of what the Lord speaks will be for our growth, encouragement, and comfort (1 Corinthians 14:3). He wants to love us and help us accept how special we are to Him.

- He may also speak to us about direction, guidance, and important decisions. This is when it becomes very important to properly discern the voice of the Lord. Discuss with your spiritual oversight and prayerfully consider any possible decisions, or changes of direction you believe God has spoken. Remember, God protects us from deception and harm by having us confirm every word by the mouth of two or three witnesses (Deuteronomy 17:6, 19:15, Hebrews 10:28).

- If we and our spiritual oversight agree that the direction and guidance in the Word is indeed from the Lord, then it is important to obey what He has told us. Disobedience can keep us from continuing to hear from Him.

How do we know when we have heard from God?

- His Voice always brings us to Jesus and exposes all sin. John heard His voice and said, "When I saw Him, I fell at His feet." (Revelations 1:17)

- His Presence (or countenance) often accompanies His voice. We may be overwhelmed and overjoyed by the glory of His presence.

- His Voice will give us scriptural assurance and will be consistent with scriptural principles.

- Whatever He speaks will be saturated with purity and unselfishness.

Questions to ask to help evaluate what you have heard:

- Does it line up with the Holy Bible, the written Scriptures?

- Does it lead us into a closer relationship with God, a greater unity with Him?

- Does it lead us into expressing love, which is putting God's benefit and the benefit of others before our own?

- Does it lead to a dying to ourselves and a greater manifestation of Christ's life in us?

- Does it cause greater humility in us and greater dependence upon God?

- Does it cause greater love, joy and peace from God in us? (This may not occur every time we listen to the Lord, but it can be a sign.)

Take time now to ask God, "What do you want to say to me right now?"

If we feel that we did not hear from God, we might want to look at some possible hindrances or blocks to hearing His Voice. Remember, one of the purposes of going through the Restoring the Foundations ministry is to be cleansed of everything that hinders our Christian walk and relationship with God. Our ability to hear God's Voice will often increase as we receive the ministry.

What can hinder us from hearing God?

- Sin, specifically pride, doubt, idols.
- Relationship with God strained through lack of communication and time in the Word.
- Distractions. If we can't be still, it will be difficult to hear His still, small voice or any of the other ways He speaks.
- God may want us to wait on Him until He is ready to talk. He will speak when He is ready. For each of us, this is a

call to persistence and patience (Psalm 25:4, 27:14, 36:9, 62:5).

- Ungodly Beliefs: "God speaks to others, but He won't speak to me." "I can't hear from God."

"FORGIVENESS IS ABOUT empowering yourself, rather than empowering your past."

T. D. Jakes

Forgiveness

Defining Forgiveness

Forgiveness is the setting of one's will, and the making of a decision to release an offending person or situation. When we forgive, we choose to set them free. By choosing to forgive we also set ourselves free. We don't hold resentment or bitterness. We let go of our plans for retaliation. We let go of feelings like they owe us something.

God has commanded that we forgive, because he loves us and wants us to lead lives of forgiveness. God has forgiven our sins and given us eternal life. He asks that we forgive those who offend us here on earth, just as He has forgiven us. Many times we cry for mercy from God because of our sin, but we are unwilling to forgive someone else for his sin. God clearly paints a picture of His opinion of forgiveness through a parable in Matthew 18:21-35. Read this passage and reflect on how God views forgiveness. He takes it very seriously.

Matthew 6:14-15 states, *"For if you forgive men their trespasses, your heavenly Father will also forgive you. But if you do not forgive men their trespasses, neither will your Father forgive your trespasses."* (NKJV)

Unforgiveness cuts off the flow of God's power and healing in our lives. Forgiveness restores His power and sets the stage for freedom and healing. It gets us in the right position to begin the healing process.

Forgiveness is setting the other person free, so we can also be free. Forgiveness releases both parties. When we hold unforgiveness, we are spiritually tied to the very thing that we hate. As we focus on the offense or offender, we re-inflict pain on ourselves over and over even when the other person may be going on with his life unfazed. The initial pain of the wrong we experience may amount to only a small fraction of the total hurt. The majority of the pain can often be avoided if we learn to deal with offenses quickly rather than to continually relive them countless times.

Forgiveness doesn't mean we will never think of the offense again, but it does mean that we won't dwell on it. As healing comes, the pain will fade and we will naturally stop thinking about the offender. Since we become whatever we focus on, God tells us to set our minds on the things of the Spirit. So, if unforgiveness goes unchecked in our life, we will eventually become like what we hate. What we cannot release, God cannot restore.

In the days of the Roman Empire, if a person killed another, the dead body was strapped to the body of the one who killed them. Over time, the decay of the dead body would begin to seep through the pores of the skin of the one who carried it. It would eventually poison the person carrying the body and he also would die. Unforgiveness is like strapping the unforgiven person to yourself. The poison of holding him in unforgiveness will seep into your own life and poison you. Forgiveness coupled with healing, allows us to de-couple some of life's painful hurts so we are no longer limited by our circumstances.

Who, What, When?

We should forgive everyone, including ourselves, others, and God. Technically, we don't forgive God because He hasn't done anything wrong. We really need to release Him of our judgment towards Him and repent of our attitude towards the Lord. We need to forgive those who have hurt us by what they have done and by what they have failed to do. We need to forgive those in authority who have wronged us. Additionally, we also need to release anything we are holding against anyone who may have already died.

Who Should Be Forgiven?

To keep our relationship right with God, we need to forgive everything, big or small. Any unforgiveness will hinder our relationship with God.

When Should We Forgive?

We need to forgive every time we are wronged or offended. We need to forgive now, or as soon as possible. Do not wait for the other party to come to us. We are not responsible for others, just for our own response.

Misconceptions And "Blocks" to Forgiveness:

- Forgiveness is a decision and not a feeling. Many times we think we have to 'feel' forgiving in order to forgive. It is important to understand that forgiveness is not limited to being a **decision only**. Forgiveness **is** a decision, but it is also a process that takes time to be fully completed, as healing comes.

- Our soul comprises our mind, will, and emotions. First, our **mind** must recognize the need for forgiveness and then we can set our **will** to forgive by making the *decision*. Our **emotions** (feelings) will eventually come into line with our decision as we receive healing.

- A common misunderstanding is that once the offender is released and forgiven, all the pain will automatically leave our hearts. This is not true. When the offense is forgiven, the healing has only just begun. We then need to come to God and allow God to heal our hearts and take away the pain. When thoughts come to mind about the situation or the offender, we need to take the thought captive and re-mind ourselves (and the enemy) that we have already for-given the offense. Do not entertain the thoughts or dwell on the offense.

- Forgiving does not mean that we deny, excuse, or ignore the offense. Forgiving isn't saying that the offense was okay or not important. Sometimes people fear that the of-fender is getting off "scot-free." Forgiving doesn't mean that the offender will not be held responsible for his actions or that there will not be consequences. However, God has said that He is our vindicator and protector. We have to release the offender from our "hook" and put him on God's "hook" so that He can deal with him in His timing. We are saying, "The offender no longer owes that debt to me; he owes it to God." This is true no matter how big the offense. God is bigger than any of our sin or any sin committed against us.

- We sometimes think that we are hurting the other person when we don't forgive, but in actuality, we are only hurting ourselves. Forgiveness does not stop someone else from causing pain; it does keep us from having to live with the pain.

- At times, we may blame God for our hurt and pain. We may even think that God caused our pain or we may won-der why He didn't prevent it from happening. God created man with free will. God will not violate man's free will even when He does not agree with man's choices. If He were to manipulate our will, we would become like robots or puppets, programmed or controlled to obey and love God. God did NOT choose the abuse, etc., but He IS here to offer healing.

20

- There is a very real enemy who is out to kill, steal and destroy everything in our lives. Our battle and struggle is not against flesh and blood, but against powers and principalities. The enemy has legal rights to torment us until we forgive. (John 10:10, Ephesians 6:12, Matthew 18:34-35)

- Some people have the misconception that we have to stay in the relationship if we forgive the offender. Forgiveness does not mean we are required to return to an unhealthy or harmful relationship or situation. Forgiveness doesn't mean that the relationship will be reconciled, although reconciliation is sometimes the result of forgiveness. Restoration and reconciliation are two separate things and take the will and desire of both people involved.

- Another block to forgiveness is to believe the lie that, "If I don't forgive, then I am protecting myself." It is possible for us to build walls out of our hurts. These walls block out both the **good** and the **bad**. They may block out further hurt, but they also block out God, love, relationships, etc. These walls can be formed when we hold unforgiveness. When we keep up our walls, these take the place of Christ because Christ is supposed to be our protection.

- Unforgiveness can be an attempt to inflict punishment on the offender or "even the score." Since thoughts of vengeance generate a sense of power, some people may resist forgiving because it means laying down a cherished defense at a time when they feel hopeless and defenseless. Sometimes a person feels that as long as he holds this unforgiveness (and probably anger as well), he has power over the other person. It may appear that this is a way to stop being a victim. However, God's Word says we have power through His Holy Spirit, not through unforgiveness.

Receiving God's Forgiveness

Sometimes it is hard to ask for and receive God's forgiveness, especially when a sin has occurred frequently. However, God is very clear in His Word that He forgives and cleanses us each time we come to Him through confession and repentance. I John 1:9 states, *"If we confess our sins, He is faithful and just to forgive us our sins and to cleanse us from all unrighteousness."* (NKJV)

God didn't put any limitations on His forgiveness, so we shouldn't either.

Asking forgiveness from God is very simple. We just get honest and real before Him about what we need and desire forgiveness for, and He will forgive us. We can come before the Lord just like David did in Psalm 32:5, *"I acknowledged my sin to You and my iniquity I did not hide. I said, 'I will confess my sin to the Lord'— then You instantly forgave me the guilt and iniquity of my sin"* (NAS).

Forgiving Yourself

Sometimes, the hardest person to forgive is ourselves. Pride says, "My sin is too big to be forgiven." It is pride that causes us to think that our sin or our problem is too big for God to handle. Unworthiness says, "I don't deserve forgiveness. I deserve to keep feeling miserable." Both pride and unworthiness try to block self-forgiveness.

We may question, "Why should I forgive myself? Isn't it enough that God forgives me?" Matthew 19:19 tells us, *"...And love your neighbor as yourself."* How can we obey this commandment? How can we walk in this love, if we do not love ourselves? To hold bitterness toward ourselves is to hold bitterness toward His beloved child. No sin is too great for the blood of Jesus to wash away. Psalm 103:12 declares, *"He has removed our rebellious acts as far as the east is from the west."* God has wiped away our guilt through Jesus and He doesn't even remember our sin any longer. He doesn't want us to continue dwelling on it either.

Remember, if we choose not to forgive ourselves, we are really saying that Jesus' dying on the Cross was not good enough or a big enough sacrifice for us!

We cannot pay for our sin through guilt or condemnation. Jesus paid the price.

Romans 8:1 says: *"There is now NO condemnation for those who are in Christ."* In other words, Christ has eliminated, canceled and ripped away our guilt.

We must let ourselves out of the prison by forgiving ourselves as well as others.

For further study see the following scriptures:

Psalm 32, 103:3; Proverbs 1:20-33; Isaiah 43:25; Matthew 18:21-35; Luke 6:37; Romans 3:23; 2 Corinthians 2:10; Colossians 3:13

Restoring the Foundations

Foundational Problem/Ministry areas

The problem/ministry areas are presented in the order they are usually approached in the ministry process. The ministry builds as we recover the legal ground that was once given over to the enemy in each of the problem/ministry areas.

First, we reclaim the ground given to the enemy due to the iniquity of our ancestors being "visited" down the family line. We call this problem/ministry area "Sins of the Fathers and Resulting Curses" or Dealing with Life's Baggage.

Then we proceed to root up any ungodly thinking that agrees with the enemy and the accompanying negative behaviors that have resulted. We want to renew our minds with God's view of things, by exchanging our Ungodly Beliefs, or lies, for Godly Beliefs.

The third area, Soul/Spirit Hurts, brings restoration to our broken hearts and healing to life's hurts. As we prayerfully wait upon the Lord, we allow Him to bring the healing we desperately need in a way only He can deliver. God wants to heal every wound and wipe away every tear, allowing us to get rid of the pain as well as various negative emotions such as resentments, anger, frustrations, rage, etc. In addition, when we expose our own sinful responses to our hurts, and when we repent of them, we recover further legal ground from the devil and/or his demons.

We are then ready for the fourth problem/ministry area, which involves casting out the demons that have used all the above-mentioned types of "legal ground" as the basis for their Demonic Oppression. This is usually easy to do after we have completed ministering to the first three problem/ministry areas. In most cases, the demons don't have "a leg to stand on" any longer because we have removed their legal ground.

"WE MUST FACE GENERATIONAL strongholds head-on. If we don't, they can remain almost unrecognizable but they don't remain benign."

Beth Moore

Dealing with Life's Baggage

Have you ever been stuck in a sin pattern and wanted to quit, but seemed to be drawn back again and again? Many people do not understand and have never been taught how the sins of their ancestors can affect and influence their lives. This chapter will show how we are "set up" for problems and influenced by our generational patterns of sins and curses. This section will also show how we are responsible for whether we sin or walk in the victory that Jesus gave to each believer through His death on the cross.

Basic Definitions

- **What is sin?** Sin is more than unwise behavior that produces sorrow and distress. It is rebellion against God. It is the breaking of God's law and instruction through disobedience.

- **What is a curse?** A curse is the penalty to be paid for the breaking of a law. The biblical meaning is the consequence that will occur because of disobedience and rebellion against God's laws.

- **What is a pattern?** A pattern is a sequence of evidences or behaviors that is repeated.

- **What is a generational sin, curse or a generational pattern?** Generational sins, curses and patterns are attitudes, actions, beliefs, behaviors, and/or habits that we have inherited from our family or relatives. We then enter into the same sin pattern and make it our own. It is usually repeated throughout our life, as well as by individuals in successive generations.

Kenneth Copeland defines curses and blessings in this way:

**"A curse is being empowered to fail.
A blessing is being empowered to succeed."**

Let's look at what the Bible says about curses.

Deuteronomy 5:9b-10 states, *"I do not leave unpunished the sins of those who hate me, but I punish the children for the sins of their parents to the third and fourth generations. But I lavish love on those who love me and obey my commands, even for a thousand generations"* (NLT).

How it works

When a person sins, that sin stands in need of being confessed. If the person doesn't confess it, then his children must confess it in order to break the generational pattern. Like an "outstanding" debt, the person's sin "hangs out there," impacting his descendants, until it is addressed through confession and cleared away. We are not required to take **responsibility** for our ancestors' sins, but we are to acknowledge and confess their sins. (We agree with God that they were wrong and that God was right.)

28

God asks us to accept responsibility for our **own sin** and to repent and be humbled. Understand that the passing down of iniquity (sin) is just that, the **passing down** of iniquity (sin). My parents' sin does not become my sin until I have made the choice to sin myself in the same way.

> **Example:** If my parents are alcoholics, it is not a sin in my life until I make the choice to begin drinking and become an alcoholic myself. The generational sin and curse pattern just means that I have a tendency to become an alcoholic, to sin in the very same way that they have sinned. It is the same with manipulation, fear, control, anger, abuse, etc. There is a spiritual pressure on me to commit the same kind of sins as my ancestors, as the curse from their sins pressures me in that direction.

A scriptural example can be found in Nehemiah 1:4-11. Nehemiah receives word that Jerusalem is again in shambles, both physically and spiritually. This burdens his heart greatly and he weeps for many days. In verse 6, Nehemiah cried out, *"I confess the sin that we Israelites, including myself and my father's house, have committed against you."* He is then granted permission to return to his homeland on a mission of restoration.

We are given a chance to stand before God and say, "These things in my life and in the lives of my ancestors are sinful and destructive. Please forgive us. Lord, I want it to stop right here, **with me**." Confession isn't about casting blame; it's about stating and acknowledging the facts.

The Bible makes it very clear that we have the power to either choose curses or blessings. Deuteronomy 30:19 says, *"Today I am giving you the <u>choice</u> between a blessing and a curse. You will be blessed if you obey the commands of the Lord your God that I am giving you today. You will receive a curse if you reject the commands of the Lord your God and turn from His ways."*

Life's Baggage
A Sample List of Generational Curses

Abandonment

Abuse: emotional, physical, mental, sexual

Addictions

Anger, rage, violence

Control, possessiveness, manipulation

Emotional dependency

Fears (all kinds)

Idolatry

Money extremes (greed, lack)

Not caring for children

Parents and children exchange roles

Physical infirmities

Pride, Rebellion

Rejection, insecurity

Religious bondage, cults

Sexual sin and perversion

Unbelief

Unworthiness, low self-esteem, inferiority, shame

Witchcraft, occult

Generational curses do not make us sin, but they can cause us to be drawn to particular types of sins. The enemy seems to know our weaknesses and those areas where we have not yet received God's healing and freedom in our lives. He also knows when we sin. Satan willingly takes advantage of any openings we give him to come against us.

Where Do Curses Come From?

Disobedience to God - God isn't out to "get us" or to curse us. Those are not His plans for us. However, God gave each one of us free will and He plainly gives us the choice of receiving blessings or curses. Curses are a natural consequence of breaking God's laws. Judgment is brought forth as His laws are broken or violated. This is the essence of the law of sowing and reaping.

The Bible clearly warns each of us that our actions have consequences. *"Don't be misled. Remember that you can't ignore God and get away with it. You will always reap what you sow! Those who live only to satisfy their own sinful desires will harvest the consequences of decay and death. But those who live to please the Spirit will harvest everlasting life from the Spirit."* (Galatians 6:7-8) (NLT)

Curses from Others / Word Curses - Many times other people bring curses into our lives. Generational sin is an example of how others can bring curses into our lives. We open our lives up to curses by agreeing with them through our own sin, choices, and beliefs. Word curses are also a way that others can affect us. Examples of word curses are statements such as, "You'll never amount to anything," and "You are a failure." The Bible tells us that there is the power of life and death in our tongue and our words. If a person receives these word curses as truth, then the curses become real in his life.

Curses from Ourselves / Self-Curses - Even sadder than having our parents or others curse us, is cursing ourselves through our own words.

Familiar examples are:

"I will probably 'blow' this job (expected failure)."

"I can't speak in front of people."

"Our family will always be poor."

"I cannot do anything right."

Personal Responsibility

People frequently ask, "Why do we have to suffer for what our relatives did?" The answer is that we don't have to if we deal with sin God's way. We will suffer only if we enter into the same sins. Although our ancestors caused us to be "set up," we are now held accountable by God for our own sins. We cannot shift the blame. The bad news is that we are affected by our parents' sins. The good news is that God has provided the way for our freedom from all the effects of their sin as well as ours.

Victory and Freedom

Some people may say, "Why do we have to go and dredge up all this stuff from the past? Didn't Jesus pay the price for the required justice?" Yes! Jesus did take the judgment and wrath of God that is due us. However, the real question is, "Have I appropriated (personally received and applied) what He did for me?" We need to receive the freedom Jesus bought for us by using God's provision. We do that by confessing the sins of our ancestors and our own sin and then breaking their power to continue to affect us. Salvation through Jesus has been available for over 2000 years, yet none of us were automatically "born again" at our birth. We must by faith receive (appropriate) salvation for ourselves.

"You were dead because of your sins and because your sinful nature was not yet cut away. Then God made you alive with Christ. He forgave all our sins. He canceled the record that contained the charges against us. He took it and destroyed it by nailing it to Christ's cross." (Colossians 2:13-14) (NLT)

The same is true for physical healing, deliverance, direction, gifts of the Spirit, love, etc. All are received by faith. Faith is believing that a promise of God applies to us and receiving that promise. Until we know about these promises and provisions, we cannot receive what Christ has provided for us. This is true for everything that we receive from God. We must receive and apply the wonderful freedoms gained for us at the Cross. Since there was no way for us to escape by our own efforts from this continuous cycle of sin and judgment, it was necessary for Christ to come and set us free.

"But Christ has rescued us from the curse pronounced by the law. When He was hung on the cross, He took upon Himself the curse for our wrongdoing." (Galatians 3:13a)

"God made Him who knew no sin to be sin for us, so that in Him we might become the righteousness of God." (2 Corinthians 5:21)

For further study see the following scriptures:

Exodus 20:1-17, 34:6-7; Leviticus 26:40; Deuteronomy 5:6-21, 24:16; 1 Kings 22:52-53; 1 Peter 1:17-19; James 3:10; 1 John 1:9

"WHEN YOU BELIEVE A LIE, you empower the liar."
Bill Johnson

Renewing Our Minds

Everyone, to some extent, lives out of wrong beliefs. Ungodly Beliefs are "lies" about ourselves, about others, and about God. They are dangerous because they affect all of our perceptions, all of our decisions, and all of our actions. It is easy to see why God wants our minds renewed.

"Don't copy the behavior and customs of this world, but let God transform you into a new person by changing the way you think. Then you will know what God wants you to do, and you will know how good and pleasing and perfect His will really is." (Romans 12:2) (NLT)

What is a belief system? It includes our beliefs, decisions, attitudes, agreements, judgments, expectations, vows, and oaths. Any beliefs that agree with God (His Word, His nature, His character, etc.) are our Godly Beliefs (GBs). Any beliefs that do not agree with God (His Word, His nature, His character, etc.) contribute to our Ungodly Beliefs (UGBs). Our beliefs affect who we are, how we perceive ourselves and how we relate to others, to the world around us, and to God. They determine how Christ-like we become, and even the quality of our Christian lives. The Ungodly Beliefs can be like a vise grip putting tight constraint on our lives, choking out the abundant life that Jesus promises.

The "perfect" Ungodly Belief is one that appears to be absolutely **TRUE** based on the **FACTS** of our experience and yet is absolutely **FALSE** based on God's Word.

Ungodly Beliefs can look like:

No one loves me.

I am all alone.

I am defective.

God doesn't love me.

Although these statements are completely false, most people who think this way do not even realize it. Until an Ungodly Belief is pointed out to us, we continue on day after day, living our life based on a lie. When we finally recognize an Ungodly Belief, we realize how completely at odds it is with God's Word.

Satan is the Author of Lies

John 8:44 says about satan, *"He was a murderer from the beginning and has always hated the truth. There is no truth in him. When he lies, it is consistent with his character; for he is a liar and the father of lies."* (NLT)

We cannot base our concept of truth on our personal experience, our "facts." There is a higher level of truth than the facts, and that is God's truth. The real truth is what He says about you and the situation.

Facts About Ungodly Beliefs and How They Are Formed

- We sometimes inherit wrong beliefs from our families or receive them from our friends or our culture.

- They are lies that have been formed in us, often since childhood, about ourselves, others and God. They are formed out of our experiences.

- Beliefs are formed from hurts, traumas, negative experiences, and words people say to us.

- Beliefs are formed from the facts of our experiences.

- An Ungodly Belief is a belief or attitude that does not agree with the Word of God, His Character, or His Nature.

Belief – Expectation Cycle

The Belief-Expectation Cycle is a very powerful tool to help you understand the impact of Ungodly Beliefs on your life.

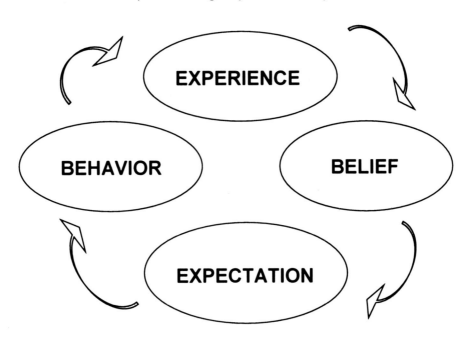

- Our beliefs are formed out of real-life experiences.

- Due to negative experiences, we form an Ungodly Belief.

- This belief causes us to expect that similar things will happen to us in the future.

- This expectation dictates our behavior, and it also affects the behavior of others.

- Our behavior can cause another similar experience that reinforces the Ungodly Belief we formed.

To better understand this cycle, consider this example:

- Experience – The teacher embarrasses you in front of others for not having the correct answer.

- Belief – Teachers are mean.

- Expectation – Teachers will always treat me that way.

- Behavior – Acting up in class and rebelling against the teachers.

The way to stop the Belief Expectation Cycle is to intervene between the experience and the belief stages of this cycle. We must choose God's truth as our new belief. When we replace the old lie with God's truth, then the other parts of the cycle will change.

Think of an example of an Ungodly Belief that has operated in your life. What experience got this belief established? What expectations and behaviors come out of this belief? Are you ready to change this belief?

Some Results of Ungodly Beliefs.

- They set us up for unhappy relationships.

- They cause distortions so that we make mountains out of mole hills.

- They cause us to take everything personally.

- They cause us to be a prisoner of put-downs or sarcasm, anger or other unhealthy patterns of relating.

- They cause us to hurt and defile those we love.

- They cause our faith to be eroded.

- They undermine our relationship with God.

- They hinder God's blessings.

- They trap us so that we don't fulfill our destiny.

- They give place for Demonic Oppression.

Belief Strongholds

Definition of a stronghold: a stronghold is anything that exalts itself, or pretends to be bigger or more powerful than God. It robs us of our focus and causes us to feel overpowered, mastered, and controlled. It consumes much of our mental and emotional energy.

Many times our Ungodly Beliefs combine with the demonic to produce an Ungodly Belief Stronghold. This stronghold underlies and reinforces all of our Ungodly Beliefs. The following strongholds are particularly vicious. As we learn about them, think about how they have affected our life.

Shame-Fear-Control, Control-Rebellion-Rejection

The Shame-Fear-Control Stronghold and the Control-Rebellion-Rejection Stronghold are a particularly common trap for many of us. These are major influences that help reinforce Ungodly Beliefs, especially Ungodly Beliefs about who we are, our very identity.

They cause a person to see himself wrongly, to have a false identity. One such network is *Shame, Fear, and Control* coupled/linked up with *Rebellion and Rejection*. It is extremely rare that one would find someone who is exhibiting one of these influences and not also find the other influences as well.

This is how they work together to bring failure into someone's life. **Shame** says, "I am bad. I am different from everyone else." **Fear** says, "I am afraid that if anybody finds out how bad I am they will not accept/approve/love me." **Control** says, "I have to control my environment and everyone in it so that no one discovers my defect."

If **Control** is threatened in any way, **Rebellion** instructs us to, "Resist, get angry, hate, scheme and strategize to regain control." As added protection, **Rejection** says, "Withdraw, so that my shame is not exposed and I am not controlled." This network might look something like this:

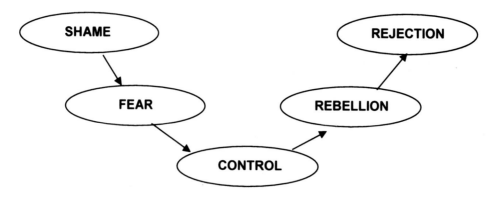

Definition of Shame: Believing, thinking, or feeling, "I am bad," "I am flawed," "I am defective," or "I am a mistake," rather than realizing the situation or choice was bad or a mistake. Shame becomes an attack on one's self, one's own identity, on "who I am."

Definition of Fear: Fear limits us, restricts us, stops us, and causes us to freeze up. Fear prevents us from opportunities and from God's best. Fear causes us to feel unprotected, unsafe, insecure, etc. Fear stems from shame as we are fearful that our shame, or our defectiveness will be exposed.

Definition of Control: Control creates a barrier between ourselves and others, as we try to control them and control ourselves so our shame will not be exposed. Control imprisons us. It promises to protect us from hurt or pain, yet it usually fails. (Control almost always stems from fear and shame.)

Definition of Rebellion: Rebellion consists of resisting direction or control, even legitimate control. Rebellion can be an open defiance or a passive resistance or unwillingness to submit to authority.

Definition of Rejection: Rejection occurs when a person believes he is unappreciated, devalued, dismissed, violated and/or victimized. Rejection can result in the person outwardly and visibly withdrawing or it can just be an inward withdrawing and hiding.

The influences of shame, fear, control, rebellion, and/or rejection are represented in every Ungodly Belief. Each influence provides an open door for the other influences in the network. The power of each influence has to be broken in order to destroy the stronghold and remove it from your life.

Breaking Free

So how do we stop thinking the way we have always thought about things? Romans 12:1-2 says don't be the way the world is and don't think the way the world thinks, but be transformed into the image of Christ by the renewing of your mind. So how do you do that?

When we think, our brain generates electrical energy that travels from neuron to neuron. As these electrical pulses travel across our brain, the neurons involved develop, creating a pathway that is even easier for the electrical pulses to follow. Thus your brain develops a system of trails or highways.

When we think a thought over and over again, that trail becomes a deep rut. Having thought the thought over and over again, it begins to affect our reasoning and becomes a part of our belief system. We eventually justify or defend our actions even though they may be ungodly. We convince ourselves that we have a good reason or right for our beliefs and resultant actions.

To break out of this downward spiral will take some determined effort. It takes time to change a direction. Just as it took time and repetition to form our Ungodly Beliefs, it takes time and repetition to replace them with our new Godly Beliefs. God has provided the way, but we have to choose it.

2 Corinthians 10:3-5 instructs us, *"to pull down strongholds, cast down imaginations, and use our spiritual weapons to come against anything that sets itself up against God and to take captive every thought that is against God."*

Ungodly Beliefs are not God's thoughts, so those thoughts are trying to put themselves above God. God and His thoughts should be what are exalted in our lives, not Ungodly Beliefs. The battleground is in the mind. We need to apply God's weapons against everything that would try to keep our thought patterns and habits in the old way. Strongholds of fear, worry, bitterness, anger, shame, control, etc. need to come down and be replaced by Christ's thoughts. Ungodly Beliefs are open doors inviting satan to come into our minds. If we don't reject satan's lies, then we accept them as truth. Isn't it awful to think that we are believing and trusting what satan says about us more than what God says about us?

II Peter 1:3-4 clearly states, *"As we know Jesus better, His divine power gives us everything we need for living a godly life. He has called us to receive his own glory and goodness! And by that same mighty power, he has given us all of his rich and wonderful promises. He has promised that you will escape the decadence all around you caused by evil desires and that you will share in his divine nature."* (NLT)

Legally Breaking Agreements

A very important part of the change process is to legally break agreements with the Ungodly Belief and to legally join in agreement with God. Then, new Godly Beliefs need to be formulated. Written Godly Beliefs help the process of removing the wrong beliefs. They help in the process of releasing ourselves from the lies and their effects. They help us release others from the constraints that our beliefs, judgments (labels), and expectations created. They help us stop permitting strongholds to develop in our minds.

For further study see the following scriptures:

Proverbs 15:4, 18:21; Mark 11:22-24; John 8:31-32; Romans 6:6-12, 10:17; Galatians 6:7-9; 2 Timothy 3:16; Hebrews 3:19; James 3:10

"GOD WANTS YOU TO BE delivered from what you have done and from what has been done to you - both are equally important to Him."

Joyce Meyer

Healing Life's Hurts

The pain of past hurts rules many lives. It simmers, it stifles, and sometimes it shuts a person completely down. However, God heals hurts. He is waiting and ready to touch our deepest pain if we will let Him. In a sense, His healing is another divine exchange, in which we offer to Him our hurt and He offers to us His healing. Psalm 147:3 states, *"He heals the brokenhearted and binds up their wounds (or sorrows)."* "Brokenhearted" refers to the wounds in the innermost portion of ourselves. Most of us do not know how to go about receiving this wonderful healing gift of God. Some of us have not been aware that this level of deep healing was available.

Definition of Soul/Spirit Hurts

Soul/Spirit Hurts are hurts to either the soul or spirit of a person that are carried and experienced within that person. They are hurts on the inside that have been suppressed and hidden. They are invisible. Soul/Spirit Hurts affect the mind, beliefs, emotions, will, relationship with God, and relationships with others.

> **Examples:** One example of a Soul/Spirit Hurt in a person's life might be when a child's parents were divorced. Another might be the hurt of a rape, or some kind of abuse. Another example might be a person being told he is fat. Each one of these hurts causes pain in a person's life, and he feels different negative emotions, and forms different Ungodly Beliefs because of them.

Sometimes our hurts come not only from what was done to us but also from what was **not** done for us. What about the toddler who was never cuddled or hugged? How about the child who was never made to feel special? Consider the teenager whose parents missed his graduation, or did not attend his birthday parties. Other hurts result from deep disappointments beyond our control: parents who failed to meet our expectations, the death of a friend or loved one, or a wanted relationship that never happened.

There are many different intensities of hurt. Some hurts are the result of a one-time incident, but some are ongoing and constant. Ongoing hurts need ongoing healing. Some of you have experienced hurts that only God knows. God cares about your hurts and wants to heal them. Let's look at some consequences of hurt.

Hurts Begin in the Family and Affect the Entire Family

The devastation of dysfunctional behavior patterns in families is widespread in many countries. In their attempt to cope with already existing pain and hurt, families develop unspoken rules that lead to the denial of feelings, problems, and reality. At the center of these rules is a belief that "it is not safe to be real." These lies create even more pain because hurts that cannot be acknowledged cannot be healed. Some unspoken lies that dysfunctional families agree to are:

- **Be Blind**: To your own perceptions of reality.

- **Be Quiet**: Do not discuss family problems with anybody.

- **Be Numb**: To your feelings and personal boundaries.

- **Be Careful**: No one can be trusted.

- **Be Good/Perfect**: It pays. It is the only safe way.

Hurts Affect the Entire Person

Hurts are like a poisonous gas seeping into every area of a person's life. Although quiet and unseen, they sap the life out of those exposed and can affect any of the following areas:

- **Physical Body:** a variety of ailments and diseases including migraines, ulcers, hives, spastic colon, and auto immune diseases.

- **Behaviors:** self-defeating behaviors that restrict personal growth and hurt others.

- **Mind:** painful flashbacks, Ungodly Beliefs, distorted perceptions and goals.

- **Emotions:** turbulent, negative emotions such as fear, hate, self-hate, anger, grief, defeat, mistrust, shame, rejection, being easily offended and feeling abandoned, helpless or hopeless.

- **Spirit:** spiritual dullness, oppression, flickering life-flow, and turning away from God.

Hurts Cause Other Hurts

Hurting people relate in ways that cause them and others around them additional hurts. Reflect on the hurts in the lives of those who have hurt you the most and observe how their hurts cause them to inflict the very same hurts onto others.

Hurts Cause Lies (UGBs) To Be Established

Hurts are a distorted lens we view life through. When we look at life through a hurt, we will most likely come away believing something that is not true. Embedded in many hurts are more lies.

Hurts Cause Ongoing Vulnerability and Hopelessness

Hurt causes us to become involved with the very things that compound the hurt. We seem to seek out and expect the very things that have caused us so much pain to happen to us again.

Hurts Cause Shame

Shame causes us to believe that we are bad, flawed, and/or disgraced. Shame can also cause us to feel like we cannot change.

Hurts Cause Defense Mechanisms

We have many different types of defenses that we use to protect ourselves from hurt. But when true healing comes, defense mechanisms become a thing of the past!

Hurts Cause Us to Wear "Masks"

Our real identity becomes unrecognizable because it is camouflaged by various defense mechanisms that we use either to express our hurt or to protect ourselves from further hurt. These behaviors are disguises, like masks, covering the real identity. Do we recognize the hurt underneath these cover-ups and disguises? God explains in Isaiah 61:1-3 and Luke 4:18-19 that Jesus came specifically to heal us and set us free from hurts and satan's lies. This healing helps us to remove our masks.

Some Common Masks:

* **Perfectionism and Performance Orientation** - We carry the deep hurt of never feeling accepted and of having to earn love and respect. We struggle to be perfect and therefore to avoid criticism while knowing deep down inside that we can never

be perfect enough. We are doomed to failure. This is a common expression of shame.

- **Anger, Blame, Criticalness, Sarcasm, and Bitterness** - We find fault with others, blaming, criticizing, and being sarcastic; hoping that by putting others down, maybe we won't feel so bad about ourselves. Anger is a symptom of feeling trapped, and/or of being violated.

- **Depression and Withdrawal** - When there is no safe place to vent our anger, when we think there is no hope of getting free from the trap around us, when we believe we have no chance of success, when we have made a mistake so great that it seems impossible even for God to correct it, it is natural to lose the spark of life, become depressed, withdraw and give up.

- **Passivity** - One way to cope is to do nothing. We feel safe if we do nothing. At least we can't be blamed for failing, or doing the wrong thing.

Hurts Cause Restricted Growth

Hurts restrict our vision of who we are and who we can become. Hurts also block intimacy in relationships, affecting whom we relate to and what we let ourselves do. Hurts are like invisible walls, holding us in and others out. They also act as invisible chains that will not let us move too far away from our hurt-distorted concept of ourselves. Hurts, the birthing place of fears, cripple our potential and keep us from becoming all that God has ordained for us to be.

Exercise: Stop for a moment and ponder these questions.

- Think of some of the hurts in your own life and how they have held you back from opportunities you might have had, but you were afraid to take the risk.

- Think of the dreams you have aborted, or only partially fulfilled.

49

- Think of people you would like to have talked to, but you couldn't because you didn't feel comfortable.

- Think of the intimacy you wanted to have in a relationship, but it never happened.

Hurts Cause Blocked Emotions

As hurts begin to pile up, we try to get rid of the pain. We may begin to separate ourselves from our pain. We block the painful emotion from our conscious awareness. Unfortunately, as we do this, many of our positive feelings are bottled up along with the negative ones. Our range of emotional expression and response eventually becomes narrower and narrower. We can become emotionally neutral, and unfeeling. We seldom feel pain, but we don't feel pleasure either. Jesus came that we might have an abundant life. Blocked and bottled-up emotions steal from us the promised abundant life Jesus died to give us.

Hurts Can Lead to Demonic Oppression

Demons gain access when our natural spiritual defenses are down due to trauma of any sort. Demons seem to work hard to engineer situations that cause hurt. Through our hurts, they can gain "legal ground." This occurs because of trauma and because of our response to the hurt. We often respond with sinful behavior out of our pain.

Anger/Disappointment Toward God

A natural result of hurt is to question God's "care" or to believe that, if He does care, He cares more about other people than about us. Someone who feels God has hurt, betrayed, or abandoned him has a difficult time expecting to receive anything good from God, particularly healing. The bottom line of the "disappointment with God issue" is a lack of trust in God. Why would the one who "hurt" you want to heal you? People carrying hurt and/or disappointment often believe that God doesn't care. This belief can form a barrier that blocks God's voice and affects the entire relationship. The serious believer has to come to terms with such unanswered questions as:

- God, where were you?

- God, if you love me so much, why didn't you intervene?

- God, why didn't you warn me not to get involved?

- God, why have I had to go through this?

- God, why don't you answer my prayers?

- God, why do you seem so far away, so hidden, so silent?

- God, why is there so much suffering in the world?

- God, why do people hurt and kill each other?

The gnawing fear that a caring God has abandoned us in our time of need must be addressed. There are several obstacles, especially in religious circles, to acknowledging this problem. Often people consider questioning God to be inappropriate, sacrilegious, ungodly, and even dangerous. We may see any attempt to work through honest, negative feelings as a lack of faith, weakness, or rebellion. A person may fear that God will be angry with him and punish him for having and expressing his real feelings. What will happen if we just bury these feelings? Our relationship with God will suffer. It will be hindered until these feelings are exposed and resolved. Until they are, we will feel as if we are merely going through Christian "motions."

A turning point occurs when we realize the root cause of our hurt is the sin in operation in the lives of other people and/or our own life. Satan is always there encouraging sin to continue. As we think about the people and situations that have hurt us the most, we can allow God to reveal to us how sin is the underlying cause. When this principle is understood, it makes it easier to stop blaming God and begin putting the blame where it belongs. God promises to be with us through the pain, the hurt, the disappointment, the things that we don't understand and the grief process not only in the past, but also in the present as we work through the pain. God doesn't always remove the pain, but He goes through it with us.

Steps to Overcoming Anger/Disappointment with God

- Recognize the true source of your hurt.

- Verbalize any anger or disappointment you experienced toward God.

- Repent of falsely accusing and blaming God.

- Allow God to redeem the hurt by speaking His love and truth into your heart.

God promises in Jeremiah 31:25 that He will fully satisfy the weary soul, and He will replenish every languishing and sorrowful person. Also, in Psalm 23:2-3 He says, *"He makes me lie down in green pastures; He leads me beside still waters. He refreshes and restores my life, and leads me in the paths of righteousness for His name's sake."* He desires wholeness and healing in the broken places of our hearts and lives. He will be faithful to do it. Will you let Him?

Other Blocks to Healing

There are other ways that we can be blocked or hindered from receiving the healing the Lord wants us to have. Consider the following items and see if any of these might be holding you back from all that God has for you.

Possible Hindrances to Healing

- Unfamiliarity with the process – I don't know what to do

- Unconfessed sin – Need to repent to God

- Unforgiveness – I think I can't / won't forgive

- Major fears – What if…

- Analytical thinking – Need to be in control all the time

- Medication – Limits our range of emotions. Consult your physician before making any changes with your medication.

- Anger/Disappointment with God – Have a wall between us and God

- Blocked emotions – Not in touch with our feelings

- Demonic blockage – Demons always want to block healing

- Unbelief – God can't/won't heal me

Pouring Out Our Complaint

When we find emotions of anger, frustration, helplessness, etc., stored inside of ourselves, it is important to release these negative emotions to the Lord. We were not designed to carry negative emotions. They need to be released so that we can receive healing in our bodies as well as our soul and spirit. God has given us permission to release these in ways that are safe for us and for others.

There are a number of examples in the scriptures when God's people "Poured Out Their Complaint" before the Lord. One excellent example is David in Psalm 142. This is a crucial part of the healing process. We are to take the innermost issues of our heart to God. His message is unmistakably real. We are to hold nothing back from our heavenly Father who already knows everything that is hidden in our hearts.

There is no formula on how to pour out your heart to God or on exactly how He will minister to you. You just need to be willing to believe and trust that God wants to touch the hurt places of your life. This is the time when God wants to do a great exchanging of joy for mourning, healing for pain, purity for shame, love for abandonment, freedom for captivity. As you are able to release your pain to the Lord, He is able to fill you with healing, His love and His truth. Remember God is not a **taker**; He is a **receiver** and a **giver**. As you **give** Him your wounds, pain, and bondage He **receives** them and in turn **gives** you liberty, healing and restoration.

Healing

Jesus is the Healer. Healing takes place as we invite Him into our situation or hurt. Sometimes we see Him and it is like a living video in which we participate. Sometimes we just sense His presence. We especially want to let Him speak to us and to hear what He has to say to us. As we encounter Him, He shows us how He sees our particular situation. He gives us the truth so we can begin to change the lies we have believed into His truth. He shows us His love and that He was there with us even when at times we didn't realize it. Sometimes He shows us His own pain about what we went through. Sometimes He helps us forgive others, or forgive ourselves. Other times, He may lovingly correct us and show us where we acted wrongly. When Jesus comes, He brings with Him the full power of the cross, forgiveness, restoration, freedom from hate, fear, anger, guilt and shame.

When we are deeply wounded, we need to continue allowing Jesus to heal our wounds, until there are no more hurts left to heal.

For further study see the following scriptures:

Exodus 15:26; 2 Chronicles 7:14; Psalm 41:4, 137:3, 147:3; Isaiah 53:3-5, 61:1-3; Jeremiah 17:14, 31:25; Luke 4:18-19; Hebrews 4:15-16

"IT IS UNSCRIPTURAL TO PRAY
for the sick if one is not
prepared also to cast out
demons. Jesus did not
separate one from the other."

Derek Prince

Freedom from Oppression

Many Christians do not realize that they can be oppressed by demons. As a result, they do nothing to stop this oppression, which leaves them at the mercy of the devil. God wants us to come into maturity in our understanding of satan and his demons. He wants us to enforce His victory over their kingdom of darkness. He wants us to know the Truth and the Truth shall make us free. He wants us to grow in maturity and faith and to appropriate His freedom by casting out the demons.

Many people question whether Christians can "have" a demon. A Christian cannot be **possessed** by demons because possession implies ownership. God tells us that we were bought with a great price, so in a sense, the question of "ownership" was settled at salvation. However, Christians can be **oppressed** by demons if they have provided any open doors or legal ground through which demons can work. To stop demonic oppression, the legal ground must be reclaimed. You will be doing this as you work through the first three problem/ministry areas of the previous sections of this book.

Demonic Oppression is the term used to represent the "pressure" exerted by demons to get us to sin, to keep us involved in sin, to blind us to God's truth and/or to keep us bound by limitations. Usually demons have an open door to gain access to us.

It is recorded on many occasions that Jesus did demonic deliverance. It was never strange or hidden. 1 John 3:8 says that Jesus came *"to destroy the works of the devil."* Jesus also passed on His ministry to His disciples. The main requirement for doing demonic deliverance is being a follower of Christ. *"And these signs shall follow them that believe; In my name they shall cast out demons; they shall speak with new tongues."* (Mark 16:17) The deliverance ministry is clear. Equally obvious is the fact that Jesus extended His authority and Name to believers to also do deliverance.

Derek Prince defined demons as, "invisible spiritual entities with minds, emotions and wills of their own, in league with and under the control of satan. They are out to do his bidding and to torment the people of God." Many Christians have allowed satan to deceive them into believing one of two major lies: that he and his demons don't exist, or that he and his demons are too powerful for Christian believers.

Either lie is devastating to the successful Christian life. These are Ungodly Beliefs that we must get rid of. See if you relate to any of the following ways that demons oppress us, working hard to destroy us and our lives.

Some Ways Demons Oppress People

Afflict   to inflict something hard to endure

Harass   to annoy or disturb persistently, to wear out by frequent attacks

Influence   to exercise indirect power over in order to sway or affect

Oppress   to lower in spirit or mood

Torment   to cause severe suffering of body or mind

Torture   to punish or coerce by inflicting excruciating pain

Worry   to disturb or destroy one's peace of mind by repeated or persistent tormenting thoughts

Wrong   to inflict injury on another without justification

The first goal of demons is to prevent us from receiving salvation. If that fails, they work to prevent Christian maturity. They try to shut us down and make us ineffective. Their chief strategy is to try to get people to turn away from God. They do this through many forms of temptation, harassment, and by challenging God and His Word. Demons lie to us and work hard to have us lie to ourselves.

Typical Influences

- **Body:** Appetites (lust, overeating, binging and purging, starvation, etc.), addictions, illnesses, sleeplessness, sleepiness, nervousness, pain, etc.

- **Soul/Mind:** Tormenting thoughts, forgetfulness, blocked memory, blocked understanding of God's Word, etc.

- **Soul/Will:** Weak will - a will that has no follow through, full of passivity.

- **Soul/Emotions:** Exaggerated emotional states: fear, anxiety, anger, panic, shame, rejection, grief that is over-extended or out of proportion, hopelessness, helplessness, etc.

- **Spirit:** Attempted prevention of salvation, spiritual lethargy, doubt of salvation experience, unbelief can affect, harass, prevent maturing, etc.

Another form of harassment is accusation and criticism. Demons will interject condemning thoughts into the minds of believers. They particularly like to stir up the past with thoughts of, "You really should have..." or "If only you had done differently." Demons are on a "seek and destroy" mission. They work together and strategize. They take advantage of our weaknesses and they love times when people are either physically and/or emotionally weak or vulnerable. They attempt to affect all areas of a person: body, soul, and spirit. They don't play fair.

Open Doors

Demons sometimes target people for special attacks, particularly those who are serious about serving God and who are advancing the kingdom of God. Demons also target people where there has been occult involvement and/or dedications in the past generations, or where the person himself has been involved in the occult. There are some very specific "open doors" by which demons frequently gain entrance into a person's life.

Common Open Doors

- Inherited Curses

- Sins of the Flesh

- Illness

- Emotional Trauma

- Passive/Trance State of Mind

- Occult Involvement

The sins of the flesh are the door that we most frequently open. This is particularly true if the sin is repeated and becomes a pattern or lifestyle of indulging the flesh.

Recognizing Demonic Influence

The following influences are extreme conditions which may indicate demonic oppression.

- Incapacity for normal living - inability to feel joy, agitation/restlessness, yo-yoing from one extreme to another

- Extreme bondage to sin - unable to stop the sin even when trying very hard

- Deception about normal personality

- Abnormal emotions - exaggerated, intense, out of control, consuming emotions

- Breakdown of marriage and family

- Tragedy and accident proneness

- Financial insufficiency - especially when the income is adequate

- Inner anguish - suicide thoughts

- Restlessness and/or insomnia

- Abnormal sex life – lust, unhealthy sexual thoughts and desires.

- Trances - "spacing out," blanking out

- Violence, super-human strength

- Demonic torment

- Self-inflicted injury – self mutilation, i.e., cutting oneself

- Functional sickness - having illness come at times that prevent Christian growth or fulfilling responsibilities.

- Unidentified foul odors

- Rapidly changing personality – Note: There are other causes for this as well

Deliverance: Some Important Keys

It is important to remember who you are in Christ. Christ has given you, as part of your identity, the authority and rule over satan and his demons. *"Behold! I have given you authority and power to trample upon serpents and scorpions and (physical and mental strength and ability) over all the power that the enemy possesses and nothing shall in any way harm you." (Luke 10:19 AMP)*

It is also important to remember who the Deliverer is! Jesus delivers us from demonic oppression. It is the power and authority through **HIM** that allows us to be free from Demonic Oppression. We command the demons to leave in the name of Jesus, a name which is above EVERY name.

"You know of Jesus of Nazareth, how God anointed Him with the Holy Spirit and with power, and how He went about doing good and healing all who were oppressed by the devil, for God was with Him." (Acts 10:38 NAS)

For further study see the following scriptures:

Mark 1:39, 5:2-13; Luke 11:20; Acts 10:38; Ephesians 6:12-18; Colossians 2:15; Hebrews 2:14-15

What Now?

You may have read Healing and Freedom because you were given this book as preparation for RTF ministry. That's great! Healing and Freedom are within sight. We encourage you to approach your RTF ministry with total abandon. Give the Holy Spirit permission to go to any place in your life He wants to go. Allow Him to go deep into the roots of your life in order to bring the most healing and freedom possible. You will not regret it because of the lasting freedom and healing that will result.

If you read Healing and Freedom and you want to know how to get help in dealing with issues in your life, that are keeping you from experiencing all that God has for you, then go to our website **www.RestoringTheFoundations.org.** Go to the Ministry Tab to the section titled, "Getting Started". You will find out more about the Restoring the Foundations ministry formats and how to schedule ministry for yourself. Don't put it off. Go there right now and see how you can receive the healing and freedom you desire.

You may feel called to become a Restoring the Foundations minister. On the website, there is a tab titled, "Training" that will explain the various ways you can become trained as an RTF minister. It is easier than you think.

If you would like to receive the RTF newsletter and receive more encouraging information like the information in this book, you can sign up on the website at the bottom of any page.

Come and join the RTF Community worldwide. We are Healing Hearts, Changing Lives, and Transforming Nations!

Contact Information:

Training@restoringthefoundations.org - for training inquiries

Healing@restoringthefoundations.org - for ministry inquiries

Office@restoringthefoundations.org - for other inquiries

Resources@restoringthefoundations.org - for other RTF resources

About Our Founders

While attending Bible school, God revealed to Chester and Betsy Kylstra the key components necessary to deal with in order to receive His healing. They, and others, only needed to satisfy His conditions of His conditional promises, applying them to the four sources from which come all of their problems. It was also important to understand the significant interrelatedness of the four sources, so that the total strategy of the enemy against them could be defeated. As they lived through and experienced His healing and restoration, they learned many Biblical principles related to healing. When the time was right, God had them begin to share what they were learning and experiencing with those around them. Out of this, the ministry of Restoring the Foundations was founded.

Chester's background included engineering and college teaching/research, Betsy's included the mental health professions. God used this preparation to grow them personally and to grow Restoring the Foundations (RTF).

Since 1990, when Chester and Betsy entered full-time ministry, God has continued to grow their hearts, lives, and vision. Their hearts were to bring God's healing into the lives of God's children. This thrust has continued, with Chester and Betsy also extending their touch to empower local churches to bring this same healing to their communities. Chester and Betsy conduct frequent seminars and conferences throughout the world to share the heart, principles, and application of Restoring the Foundations Ministry. As a result, there is a significant and growing family of ministry teams and trainers world-wide. Restoring the

Foundations has nearly 300 ministers in the Healing House Network in 18 nations around the world, as well as tens of thousands of trained lay ministers ministering in their local churches.

In 2004 God led Chester and Betsy to start a training center to further pass on the RTF revelation. They were led through a prophetic journey to purchase Echo Mountain Inn in Hendersonville, North Carolina. This facility became the new world headquarters and the International Training Center for Restoring the Foundations.

The ministry of Restoring the Foundations continues to expand around the world because two people were wiling to say "Yes" to Father God. Thousands have received personal healing, marriages have been restored, families have been reconciled. Many have been empowered and released into their God given purpose and destiny because of Restoring the Foundations ministry.

Restoring the Foundations is Healing Hearts, Changing Lives and Transforming Nations…One Life at a Time.

CPSIA information can be obtained
at www.ICGtesting.com
Printed in the USA
FFOW03n0038310518
46990293-49257FF